FAMILY LINES

FAMILY LINES

FAMILY LINES

Poems About Parents and Parenthood

edited by

SIMON ARMITAGE
& RACHEL BOWER

faber

First published in 2026
by Faber & Faber Ltd
The Bindery, 51 Hatton Garden
London, EC1N 8HN

Typeset by Typo•glyphix, Burton-on-Trent, DE14 3HE
Printed by Short Run Press

A CIP record for this book
is available from the British Library

ISBN 978-0-571-36504-3

Printed and bound in the UK on FSC® certified paper in line with our continuing
commitment to ethical business practices, sustainability and the environment.
For further information see faber.co.uk/environmental-policy

Our authorised representative in the EU for product safety is
Easy Access System Europe, Mustamäe tee 50, 10621 Tallinn, Estonia
gpsr.requests@easproject.com

2 4 6 8 10 9 7 5 3 1

CONTENTS

'I crossed the border into the Republic of Motherhood'
BEGINNINGS AND EARLY DAYS

'Let the rivers pour over my head'
ABSENCE AND LOSS

'A kind of faith prevails'
GROWING UP AND LETTING GO

'To thee my lay is due'
MOTHERS AND MOTHER FIGURES

'Only a dad with a tired face'
FATHERS AND FATHER FIGURES

'We her children hold on like drought holds out for rain'
CHANGE AND AGEING

'& the whole garden will bow'
FAREWELLS AND RENEWAL

FOREWORD

This anthology opens with the invisible flicker of new life in Maura Dooley's 'Freight' and closes, full circle, with Thomas Hardy's powerful poem 'Heredity', which describes how 'trait and trace' live on, even after death. We all come from somewhere, a mysterious fact poets have been exploring for millennia in poems about parents, parenting and parenthood – yet this subject remains as much a puzzle, amazement and source of sorrow as it always has.

These thoughts formed part of a conversation between the editors of this book after a poetry workshop at the University of Leeds one cold October evening back in 2018. Simon and I had shared poems about parents and parenthood, some of which you will find in this book, including Tony Harrison's devastating poem about his mother's last apple pie, Seamus Heaney's evocation of the 'stale smoke and oxter-sweat' on his father's old suits and Sharon Olds's visceral account of labour and birth. After the workshop, Simon and I discussed how we'd love to find a book that captured the long and diverse history of poems about parenthood, situating the flourishing body of contemporary poems within a broader context. And so this anthology was born.

The poems in *Family Lines* are testimonies to the relationships and domestic moments that shape and make (and unmake) us. Although the book largely follows the arc of birth, life and death, there is no single journey here. There are overlaps and complexities; many poems are about being a parent and a child at the same time, for instance. Lucille Clifton's 'the lost baby poem' and Ben Jonson's 'On My First Son' speak of absence and loss, while poems such as Fleur Adcock's 'For a Five-Year-Old' and Ted Hughes's 'Full Moon and Little Frieda' offer the wonder and accompanying shift in outlook that a young child can bring to our world. Families and parenting obviously come in many different forms. This book seeks to capture as diverse a range of voices and viewpoints as possible within the space available, from Liz Berry's bewildering 'wild queendom' of early motherhood to the painful questions of affiliation and filiation raised by Jackie Kay's 'Chapter 2: The Original Birth Certificate' to the tender memories of the father in Roger Robinson's 'Sleep'.

The biggest challenge has been whittling the vast wealth of rich material down to the selection of exceptional poems you have in your hand. This book includes many great, powerful poems by writers whose names will be familiar – William Shakespeare, W. B. Yeats, Elizabeth Barrett Browning – but there are also many less familiar, equally extraordinary poems about parenthood by contemporary writers. We are keen to approach the subject with a fresh perspective, and this means that several of our choices differ from those of other anthologies. We made the decision, for example, to leave out Philip Larkin's much-anthologised 'This Be the Verse' in order to make room for his lesser-known 'Mother, Summer, I'. This moving poem sits alongside other poems concerning mothers by writers ranging from Christina Rossetti and Robert Louis Stevenson to Selima Hill and Mary Jean Chan.

We were surprised by the urgency with which historical poems spoke to our present moment. Together in dialogue with more recent poems, they bear witness to the relationships that make us who we are. We hope our selection shows how the poetry of parenthood not only considers children and parents but, more fundamentally, what it means to be alive: to live and love and grieve. The intention is to start a conversation – to prompt questions – about how we relate to others and what it means to be human.

You will discover instances of deep connection and joy in this book, but the poems do not shy away from pain and despair. *Family Lines* covers themes of identity and belonging, new bodies and old, love and loss. It is a book to pick up at key moments in family life. We hope that you find what you need here.

RACHEL BOWER, 2026

'I am the ship in which you sail'

———————

PREGNANCY AND EXPECTATIONS

MAURA DOOLEY
Freight

I am the ship in which you sail,
little dancing bones,
your passage between the dream
and the waking dream,
your sieve, your pea-green boat.
I'll pay whatever toll your ferry needs.
And you, whose history's already charted
in a rope of cells, be tender to
those other unnamed vessels
who will surprise you one day,
tug-tugging, irresistible,
and float you out beyond your depth,
where you'll look down, puzzled, amazed.

ANNA LÆTITIA BARBAULD
To a Little Invisible Being Who Is Expected Soon to Become Visible

Germ of new life, whose powers expanding slow
For many a moon their full perfection wait,—
Haste, precious pledge of happy love, to go
Auspicious borne through life's mysterious gate.

What powers lie folded in thy curious frame,—
Senses from objects locked, and mind from thought!
How little canst thou guess thy lofty claim
To grasp at all the worlds the Almighty wrought!

And see, the genial season's warmth to share,
Fresh younglings shoot, and opening roses glow!
Swarms of new life exulting fill the air,—
Haste, infant bud of being, haste to blow!

For thee the nurse prepares her lulling songs,
The eager matrons count the lingering day;
But far the most thy anxious parent longs
On thy soft cheek a mother's kiss to lay.

She only asks to lay her burden down,
That her glad arms that burden may resume;
And nature's sharpest pangs her wishes crown,
That free thee living from thy living tomb.

She longs to fold to her maternal breast
Part of herself, yet to herself unknown;
To see and to salute the stranger guest,
Fed with her life through many a tedious moon.

Come, reap thy rich inheritance of love!

CAROLINE BIRD
Primitive Heart

You are the size of an orange seed and
developing a heart. Same, baby, same.
Your pre-heart is made of two tubes
which must fuse together now into one
primitive structure. Tell me about it.
By Friday your neural groove will herald
the beginning of your brain. Snap.
I'm a chickpea, bud, a tadpole,

pre-me. Within a week you'll double
in scope. I can't compete with that level
of personal growth. You'll outdo me, pip.
I'm unfused. Sketchy. Two heart strings
fumbling to combine. I'm not supposed to
dread completion, baby, am I? Yours nor mine.

GENEVIEVE TAGGARD
With Child

Now I am slow and placid, fond of sun,
Like a sleek beast, or a worn one:
No slim and languid girl – not glad
With the windy trip I once had,
But velvet-footed, musing of my own,
Torpid, mellow, stupid as a stone.

You cleft me with your beauty's pulse, and now
Your pulse has taken body. Care not how
The old grace goes, how heavy I am grown,
Big with this loneliness, how you alone
Ponder our love. Touch my feet and feel
How earth tingles, teeming at my heel!
Earth's urge, not mine, – my little death, not hers;
And the pure beauty yearns and stirs.

It does not heed our ecstacies, it turns
With secrets of its own, its own concerns,
Toward a windy world of its own, toward stark
And solitary places. In the dark
Defiant even now; it tugs and moans
To be untangled from these mother's bones.

GEORGIA DOUGLAS JOHNSON
Black Woman

Don't knock at my door, little child,
    I cannot let you in,
You know not what a world this is
    Of cruelty and sin.
Wait in the still eternity
    Until I come to you,
The world is cruel, cruel, child,
    I cannot let you in!

Don't knock at my heart, little one,
    I cannot bear the pain
Of turning deaf-ear to your call
    Time and time again!
You do not know the monster men
    Inhabiting the earth,
Be still, be still, my precious child,
    I must not give you birth!

ALDEN NOWLAN
It's Good To Be Here

I'm in trouble, she said
to him. That was the first
time in history that anyone
had ever spoken of me.

It was 1932 when she
was just fourteen years old
and men like him
worked all day for
one stinking dollar.

There's quinine, she said.
That's bullshit, he told her.

Then she cried and then
for a long time neither of them
said anything at all and then
their voices kept rising until
they were screaming at each other
and then there was another long silence and then
they began to talk very quietly and at last he said
well, I guess we'll just have to make the best of it.

While I lay curled up,
my heart beating,
in the darkness inside her.

GAIL McCONNELL
Orange

There must be many ways to peel an orange. And by orange I mean Tangerine. Or Clementine. The pocket-sized fruits best not pocket-stored. With these one can fashion a spiral. Or: witness the teenage boy make testes and a penis before segmenting the fruit. With the orange itself, you're into the business of marking the skin – the knife's continuous line – then peeling it back to reveal the flesh and pulling it off in great husks, the cuts on your palms all stinging. 'I have worked myself too dry this time. There is not one idea left in the orange.' So wrote Woolf as though thinking of Ponge, who sees the orange seed as a miniature lemon.

We broach it first in bed, this question of sperm. You rule out Danish blondes. Alone, I tick things in the pull-down menus. Caucasian. Dark hair. Green eyes. Five five to five nine. Fermin appears. His true name I'll never know. It takes me back to the three-legged cat we had in Georgia, Mr Joshua Ingalls. When the time came to cross the sea, we took him to the shelter. They renamed him Fiesta. He is Spanish. He does not use prescription lenses. He does not suffer from any allergies, medical conditions or physical abnormalities. I listen to his voice. I see his baby photos. I read his handwriting, profile, Q&A, Emotional Intelligence Test, family tree. He is a saint. He rolls an orange – Navel, say, or Blood. He rolls it round. Round beneath his palm as the bulls run through the streets. It's alphabetical, I know. After Fiesta, Guy or Gabriella or Giggles. But seeing meaning in the sequence can be hard to resist. The first orange tree in

France came from Pamplona. This fact I give you with a glass of juice. I have read too much and wish I could unknow the things I seem to know. To hold.

Why does the mother hate her child? Winnicott starts an alphabet, beating Mr Ramsay and making it to R. 'His excited love is cupboard love, so that having got what he wants he throws her away like orange peel.' It is morning. As my lover opens her mouth, making the awww sounding shape I thought might be orange, I see it might be ovum. What can I give her, having neither seed nor egg, or not the egg she needs? Do I want to be the mother thrown away like orange peel? Will I be so hated and, withstanding it, so loved? Or will I be a different mother, whose body has not been a room, whose breasts contain no nourishment, who feeds our child with Honeybells, Tangelos, Satsumas, Mandarins, Lane Lates, Summer Golds, Cara Caras? Child, if you come, you will be twice loved. My love will carry you, and I will be the one who peels for you the Minneola, gives you it in segments.

JAN-HENRY GRAY
April 1984

The young mother   born
    with the wrong name
        boards a plane.
Flanked by
     her second   and   third child,
she squeezes the last
    of the honey from the plastic packet
and stirs
     her tea
      not   with the flimsy stick
           handed to her   by the pink stewardess
but with her own stubborn finger
    ignorant   of etiquette   or the gossip
      gathering in the rows behind her.

The young mother   does not check
      her watch
     during any   of the   19 hours
        her first flight   her first time
    over the Pacific Ocean—
      that blue expanse on the map from
        Manila to Milkenhoney, California.

She watches white
    cartoon clouds
     out of the oval window
   practices her English
    wiggles in the heat of
     her cloth corset   to hide her size

and keeps   a flat hand
    on her belly
    as if to say
        soon   enough   soon enough.

                            In three weeks, her last child,
        small-eyed   his skin   lighter than the others
will be born:
        he will hear   the clatter   of two languages
            stories   about home   from the others and
        cry for his mother's milk.

'I think I'm going to have it'

BIRTHS AND ARRIVALS

ANNE STEVENSON
Poem for a Daughter

'I think I'm going to have it,'
I said, joking between pains.
The midwife rolled competent
sleeves over corpulent milky arms.
'Dear, you never have it,
we deliver it.'
A judgement years proved true.
Certainly I've never had you

as you still have me, Caroline.
Why does a mother need a daughter?
Heart's needle, hostage to fortune,
freedom's end. Yet nothing's more perfect
than that bleating, razor-shaped cry
that delivers a mother to her baby.
The bloodcord snaps that held
their sphere together. The child,
tiny and alone, creates the mother.

A woman's life is her own
until it is taken away
by a first particular cry.
Then she is not alone
but parts of the premises
of everything there is:
a time, a tribe, a war.
When we belong to the world
we become what we are.

RACHEL RICHARDSON
Shearwater

You were given feet but had never touched
them to earth. You were given the sea
and you fed upon it for months.

So when your head crowned, ashen
with loss of blood from the cord
wound tight around your neck,

and when they cut you from me,
and you were silent, and the tide in me
receded, I remembered the shearwaters

following the ship—the slow sweep
of them riding the wind's current.
The stretch of them, hovering,

cruciform, shearing the air the way an envelope
slides back into a box of letters, making
its narrow space. I had watched

from the stern for hours their trailing:
as if stillness itself drifted toward me.
I thought it was my life.

Then someone lifted you up,
and there was a sound,
and they laid you on me, breathing.

SHARON OLDS
First Birth

I had thought so little, really, of *her*,
inside me, all that time, not breathing –
intelligent, maybe curious,
her eyes closed. When the vagina opened,
slowly, from within, from the top, my eyes
rounded in shock and awe, it was like being
entered for the first time, but entered
from the inside, the child coming in
from the other world. Enormous, stately,
she was pressed through the channel, she turned, and rose,
they held her up by a very small ankle,
she dangled indigo and scarlet, and spread
her arms out in this world. Each thing
I did, then, I did for the first
time, touched the flesh of our flesh,
brought the tiny mouth to my breast,
she drew the avalanche of milk
down off the mountain, I felt as if
I was nothing, no one, I was everything to her, I was hers.

PASCALE PETIT
Escape

I pushed headfirst into the light
through the nine circles of your cervix,

then rested, my face free of you.
You gripped my shoulders.

You were a stone I had to crawl out of.
But there was this air I wanted to breathe,

clouds of it floating in the colour-room
where cold voices cut my skin.

I must have been tunnelling for months,
planning escape-routes

in those new mazes of my brain.
There was a hole in my head

through which I could hear the stars singing.
The seal over my lips cracked

as I tried to sing back.
Angels drew out my legs

and washed you off me.
I was not yet your daughter. You

would never be my mother.
Those threats you whispered

as I lay helpless inside you
were in no mother tongue.

The moment my feet left you
I started to worship the world.

ALFRED, LORD TENNYSON
De Profundis

Out of the deep, my child, out of the deep,
Where all that was to be, in all that was,
Whirl'd for a million aeons thro' the vast
Waste dawn of multitudinous-eddying light –
Out of the deep, my child, out of the deep,
Thro' all this changing world of changeless law,
And every phase of ever-heightening life,
And nine long months of antenatal gloom,
With this last moon, this crescent – her dark orb
Touch'd with earth's light – thou comest, darling boy;
Our own; a babe in lineament and limb
Perfect, and prophet of the perfect man;
Whose face and form are hers and mine in one,
Indissolubly married like our love;
Live, and be happy in thyself, and serve
This mortal race thy kin so well, that men
May bless thee as we bless thee, O young life
Breaking with laughter from the dark; and may
The fated channel where thy motion lives
Be prosperously shaped, and sway thy course
Along the years of haste and random youth
Unshatter'd; then full-current thro' full man;
And last in kindly curves, with gentlest fall,
By quiet fields, a slowly-dying power,
To that last deep where we and thou are still.

SAMUEL LAYCOCK
Welcome, Bonny Brid!

Tha 'rt welcome, little bonny brid,
But should n't ha' come just when tha did;
    Toimes are bad.
We 're short o' pobbies for eawr Joe,
But that, of course, tha did n't know,
    Did ta, lad?

Aw 've often yeard mi feyther tell,
'At when aw coom i' th' world misel
    Trade wur slack;
An' neaw it 's hard wark pooin' throo—
But aw munno fear thee; iv aw do
    Tha 'll go back.

Cheer up! these toimes 'ull awter soon;
Aw 'm beawn to beigh another spoon—
    One for thee;
An' as tha 's sich a pratty face,
Aw 'll let thee have eawr Charley's place
    On mi knee.

God bless thee, love, aw 'm fain tha 'rt come,
Just try an' mak thisel awhoam:
    What ar 't co'd?
Tha 'rt loike thi mother to a tee,
But tha 's thi feyther's nose, aw see,
    Well, aw 'm blow'd!

Come, come, tha need n't look so shy,
Aw am no' blackin' thee, not I;
    Settle deawn,
An' tak this haup'ney for thisel',
There 's lots o' sugar-sticks to sell
    Deawn i' th' teawn.

Aw know when furst aw coom to th' leet
Aw 're fond o' owt 'at tasted sweet;
    Tha 'll be th' same.
But come, tha 's never towd thi dad
What he 's to co thi yet, mi lad—
    What 's thi name?

Hush! hush! tha munno cry this way,
But get this sope o' cinder tay
    While it 's warm;
Mi mother us'd to give it me,
When aw wur sich a lad as thee,
    In her arm.

Hush a babby, hush a bee—
Oh, what a temper! dear a-me,
    Heaw tha skroikes!
Here 's a bit o' sugar, sithee;
Howd thi noise, an' then aw 'll gie thee
    Owt tha loikes.

We 'n nobbut getten coarsish fare,
But eawt o' this tha 'st ha' thi share,
    Never fear.

Aw hope tha 'll never want a meel,
But allus fill thi bally weel
    While tha 'rt here.

Thi feyther 's noan bin wed so long,
An' yet tha sees he 's middlin' throng
    Wi' yo' o:
Besides thi little brother, Ted,
We 'n one up-steers, asleep i' bed
    Wi' eawr Joe.

But though we 'n childer two or three,
We 'll make' a bit o' reawm for thee—
    Bless thee, lad!
Tha 'rt th' prattiest brid we han i' th' nest;
Come, hutch up closer to mi breast—
    Aw 'm thi dad.

JACKIE KAY
Chapter 2: The Original Birth Certificate

I say to the man at the desk
I'd like my original birth certificate
Do you have any idea what your name was?
Close, close he laughs. *Well what was it?*

So slow as torture he discloses bit by bit
my mother's name, my original name
the hospital I was born in, the time I came.

Outside Edinburgh is soaked in sunshine
I talk to myself walking past the castle.
So, so, so, I was a midnight baby after all.

**I am nineteen
my whole life is changing**

On the first night
I see her shuttered eyes in my dreams

**I cannot pretend she's never been
my stitches pull and threaten to snap**

**my own body a witness
leaking blood to sheets, milk to shirts**

On the second night
I'll suffocate her with a feather pillow

Bury her under a weeping willow
Or take her far out to sea

and watch her tiny eight-pound body
sink to shells and reshape herself.

So much the better than her body
encased in glass like a museum piece

On the third night
I toss I did not go through these months

for you to die on me now
on the third night I lie

willing life into her
breathing air all the way down the corridor

to the glass cot
I push my nipples through

NAN COHEN
A Newborn Girl at Passover

Consider one apricot in a basket of them.
It is very much like all the other apricots—
an individual already, skin and seed.

Now think of this day. One you will probably forget.
The next breath you take, a long drink of air.
Holiday or not, it doesn't matter.

A child is born and doesn't know what day it is.
The particular joy in my heart she cannot imagine.
The taste of apricots is in store for her.

'I crossed the border into the
Republic of Motherhood'

———————

BEGINNINGS AND EARLY DAYS

SYLVIA PLATH
Morning Song

Love set you going like a fat gold watch.
The midwife slapped your footsoles, and your bald cry
Took its place among the elements.

Our voices echo, magnifying your arrival. New statue.
In a drafty museum, your nakedness
Shadows our safety. We stand round blankly as walls.

I'm no more your mother
Than the cloud that distils a mirror to reflect its own slow
Effacement at the wind's hand.

All night your moth-breath
Flickers among the flat pink roses. I wake to listen:
A far sea moves in my ear.

One cry, and I stumble from bed, cow-heavy and floral
In my Victorian nightgown.
Your mouth opens clean as a cat's. The window square

Whitens and swallows its dull stars. And now you try
Your handful of notes;
The clear vowels rise like balloons.

HOLLIE McNISH
After Party / After Birth

written aged 27

where were the balloons?
where were the party poppers?
where was the human tunnel
holding hands above our heads?

where was the champagne popped
sprayed straight into our mouths?
where were the crowd claps quickening
as we stepped outside with her?

where were the well done badges
slapped onto our tops?
where were the banners painted gold?
where were the silver trays of vol-au-vents?

where were the speeches and the toasts?
where were the three cheers for us?
where were the stamps and the shouts
and the claps and the fuss?
where was the drum parade?
the brass band?
the trombones?
the tambourines?
the pom-poms?
the three-tiered cake?
the horse and cart?
the limousine?

i *know* it's not a wedding
but did you not see what we did?
do you not get how hard that was?
did no one see me push; him pull?
does no one smell our sweat, my blood?
does no one know how much that hurt?
you are all just walking round
as if it's one more day on earth!

where are the balloons?
where are the clapping, waving crowds?
a welcome to this planet sign?
a prosecco as we all step out?

just a well done would be nice
at least hand us both a fizzy drink
one balloon strapped to our fucking car
to acknowledge what this is

ROBERT BURNS
A Poet's Welcome to His Love-Begotten Daughter

Thou's welcome, Wean! Mishanter fa' me,
If thoughts o' thee, or yet thy Mamie,
Shall ever daunton me or awe me,
My sweet, wee lady;
Or if I blush when thou shalt ca' me
Tyta, or Daddie.

Tho' now they ca'me Fornicator,
An' tease my name in kintra clatter,
The mair they talk, I'm kend the better;
E'en let them clash!
An auld wife's tongue's a feckless matter
To gie ane fash.

Welcome! My bonie, sweet, wee Dochter!
Tho' ye come here a wee unsought for;
And tho' your comin I hae fought for,
Baith Kirk and Queir;
Yet by my faith, ye're no unwrought for,
That I shall swear!

Wee image o' my bonie Betty,
As fatherly I kiss and daut thee,
As dear and near my heart I set thee,
Wi' as gude will,
As a' the Priests had seen me get thee
That's out o' Hell.

Sweet fruit o' monie a merry dint,
My funny toil is no a' tint;
Tho' thou cam to the warld asklent,
Which fools may scoff at,
In my last plack thy part's be in't,
The better half o't.

Tho' I should be the waur bestead,
Thou's be as braw and bienly clad,
And thy young years as nicely bred
Wi' education,
As onie brat o' Wedlock's bed
In a' thy station.

Gude grant that thou may ay inherit
Thy Mither's looks an' gracefu' merit;
An' thy poor, worthless Daddie's spirit,
Without his failins!
'Twill please me mair to see thee heir it
Than stocket mailins!

For if thou be, what I wad hae thee,
An' tak the counsel I shall gie thee,
I'll never rue my trouble wi' thee,
The cost nor shame o't,
But be a loving Father to thee,
And brag the name o't.

SAMUEL TAYLOR COLERIDGE
Sonnet: On Receiving a Letter Informing Me of the Birth of a Son

When they did greet me Father, sudden Awe
Weigh'd down my spirit! I retired and knelt
Seeking the throne of grace, but inly felt
No heavenly visitation upwards draw
My feeble mind, nor cheering ray impart.
Ah me! before the Eternal Sire I brought
The unquiet silence of confused Thought
And shapeless feelings: my o'erwhelmed Heart
Trembled: & vacant tears stream'd down my face.
And now once more, O Lord! to thee I bend,
Lover of souls! and groan for future grace,
That, ere my Babe youth's perilous maze have trod,
Thy overshadowing Spirit may descend
And he be born again, a child of God!

LIZ BERRY
The Republic of Motherhood

I crossed the border into the Republic of Motherhood
and found it a queendom, a wild queendom.
I handed over my clothes and took its uniform,
its dressing gown and undergarments, a cardigan
soft as a creature, smelling of birth and milk,
and I lay down in Motherhood's bed, the bed I had made
but could not sleep in, for I was called at once to work
in the factory of Motherhood. The owl shift,
the graveyard shift. Feedingcleaninglovingfeeding.
I walked home, heartsore, through pale streets,
the coins of Motherhood singing in my pockets.
Then I soaked my spindled bones
in the chill municipal baths of Motherhood,
watching strands of my hair float from my fingers.
Each day I pushed my pram through freeze and blossom
down the wide boulevards of Motherhood
where poplars bent their branches to stroke my brow.
I stood with my sisters in the queues of Motherhood –
the weighing clinic, the supermarket – waiting
for its bureaucracies to open their doors.
As required, I stood beneath the flag of Motherhood
and opened my mouth although I did not know the anthem.
When darkness fell I pushed my pram home again,
by lamp-light wrote urgent letters of complaint
to the Department of Motherhood but received no response.
I grew sick and was healed in the hospitals of Motherhood
with their long-closed isolation wards
and narrow beds watched over by a fat moon.
The doctors were slender and efficient

and when I was well they gave me my pram again
so I could stare at the daffodils in the parks of Motherhood
while winds pierced my breasts like silver arrows.
In snowfall, I haunted Motherhood's cemeteries,
the sweet fallen beneath my feet –
Our Lady of the Birth Trauma, Our Lady of Psychosis.
I wanted to speak to them, tell them I understood,
but the words came out scrambled, so I knelt instead
and prayed in the chapel of Motherhood, prayed
for that whole wild fucking queendom,
its sorrow, its unbearable skinless beauty,
and all the souls that were in it. I prayed and prayed
until my voice was a nightcry,
sunlight pixellating my face like a kaleidoscope.

JOANNA BAILLIE
A Mother to Her Waking Infant

Now in thy dazzling half-oped eye,
Thy curled nose and lip awry,
Uphoisted arms and noddling head,
And little chin with crystal spread,
Poor helpless thing! what do I see,
That I should sing of thee?

From thy poor tongue no accents come,
Which can but rub thy toothless gum:
Small understanding boasts thy face,
Thy shapeless limbs nor step nor grace:
A few short words thy feats may tell,
And yet I love thee well.

When wakes the sudden bitter shriek,
And redder swells thy little cheek
When rattled keys thy woes beguile,
And through thine eyelids gleams the smile,
Still for thy weakly self is spent
Thy little silly plaint.

But when thy friends are in distress.
Thou'lt laugh and chuckle n'ertheless,
Nor with kind sympathy be smitten,
Though all are sad but thee and kitten;
Yet puny varlet that thou art,
Thou twitchest at the heart.

Thy smooth round cheek so soft and warm;
Thy pinky hand and dimpled arm;
Thy silken locks that scantly peep,
With gold tipped ends, where circle deep,
Around thy neck in harmless grace,
So soft and sleekly hold their place,
Might harder hearts with kindness fill,
And gain our right goodwill.

Each passing clown bestows his blessing,
Thy mouth is worn with old wives' kissing;
E'en lighter looks the gloomy eye
Of surly sense when thou art by;
And yet, I think, whoe'er they be,
They love thee not like me.

Perhaps when time shall add a few
Short years to thee, thou'lt love me too;
And after that, through life's long way,
Become my sure and cheering stay;
Wilt care for me and be my hold,
When I am weak and old.

Thou'lt listen to my lengthened tale,
And pity me when I am frail—
But see, the sweepy spinning fly
Upon the window takes thine eye.
Go to thy little senseless play;
Thou dost not heed my lay.

EAVAN BOLAND
Night Feed

This is dawn.
Believe me
This is your season, little daughter:
The moment daisies open,
The hour mercurial rainwater
Makes a mirror for sparrows.
It's time we drowned our sorrows.

I tiptoe in.
I lift you up
Wriggling
In your rosy, zipped sleeper.
Yes this is the hour
For the early bird and me
When finder is keeper.

I crook the bottle.
How you suckle!
This is the best I can be:
Housewife
To this nursery
Where you hold on,
Dear life.

A silt of milk.
The last suck.
And now your eyes are open
Birth-coloured and offended.

Earth wakes.
You go back to sleep.
The feed is ended.

Worms turn.
Stars go in.
Even the moon is losing face.
Poplars stilt for dawn
And we begin
The long fall from grace.
I tuck you in.

ALICE MEYNELL
Cradle Song at Twilight

The child not yet is lulled to rest.
Too young a nurse, the slender Night
So laxly holds him to her breast
That throbs with flight.

He plays with her, and will not sleep.
For other playfellows she sighs;
An unmaternal fondness keep
Her alien eyes.

HELEN DUNMORE
Patrick I

Patrick, I cannot write
such poems for you as a father might
coming upon your smile,

your mouth, half sucking, half sleeping,
your tears shaken from your eyes like sparklers
break up the nightless weeks of your life:

lightheaded, I go to the kitchen
and cook breakfast, aching as you grow hungry.
Mornings are plain as the pages
of books in sedentary schooldays.

If I were eighty and lived next door
hanging my pale chemises on the porch
would I envy or pity my neighbour?

Polished and still as driftwood
she stands smoothing her dahlias;

liquid, leaking,
I cup the baby's head to my shoulder:

the child's a boy and will not share
one day these obstinate, exhausted mornings.

RITA DOVE
Daystar

She wanted a little room for thinking;
but she saw diapers steaming on the line,
a doll slumped behind the door.

So she lugged a chair behind the garage
to sit out the children's naps.

Sometimes there were things to watch –
the pinched armor of a vanished cricket,
a floating maple leaf. Other days
she stared until she was assured
when she closed her eyes
she'd see only her own vivid blood.

She had an hour, at best, before Liza appeared
pouting from the top of the stairs.
And just what was mother doing
out back with the field mice? Why,

building a palace. Later
that night when Thomas rolled over and
lurched into her, she would open her eyes
and think of the place that was hers
for an hour – where
she was nothing,
pure nothing, in the middle of the day.

KATHLEEN JAMIE
February

To the heap of nappies
carried from the automatic
in a red plastic basket

to the hanging out, my mouth
crowded with pegs;
to the notched prop

hoisting the wash,
a rare flight of swans,
hills still courying snow;

to spring's hint sailing
the westerly, snowdrops
sheltered by rowans –

to the day of St Bride, the first
sweet-wild weeks of your life
I willingly surrender.

DON PATERSON
Waking with Russell

Whatever the difference is, it all began
the day we woke up face-to-face like lovers
and his four-day-old smile dawned on him again,
possessed him, till it would not fall or waver;
and I pitched back not my old hard-pressed grin
but his own smile, or one I'd rediscovered.
Dear son, I was *mezzo del cammin*
and the true path was as lost to me as ever
when you cut in front and lit it as you ran.
See how the true gift never leaves the giver:
returned and redelivered, it rolled on
until the smile poured through us like a river.
How fine, I thought, this waking amongst men!
I kissed your mouth and pledged myself forever.

W. B. YEATS
A Prayer for my Daughter

Once more the storm is howling, and half hid
Under this cradle-hood and coverlid
My child sleeps on. There is no obstacle
But Gregory's wood and one bare hill
Whereby the haystack- and roof-levelling wind,
Bred on the Atlantic, can be stayed;
And for an hour I have walked and prayed
Because of the great gloom that is in my mind.

I have walked and prayed for this young child an hour
And heard the sea-wind scream upon the tower,
And under the arches of the bridge, and scream
In the elms above the flooded stream;
Imagining in excited reverie
That the future years had come,
Dancing to a frenzied drum,
Out of the murderous innocence of the sea.

May she be granted beauty and yet not
Beauty to make a stranger's eye distraught,
Or hers before a looking-glass, for such,
Being made beautiful overmuch,
Consider beauty a sufficient end,
Lose natural kindness and maybe
The heart-revealing intimacy
That chooses right, and never find a friend.

Helen being chosen found life flat and dull
And later had much trouble from a fool,
While that great Queen, that rose out of the spray,
Being fatherless could have her way
Yet chose a bandy-legged smith for man.
It's certain that fine women eat
A crazy salad with their meat
Whereby the Horn of Plenty is undone.

In courtesy I'd have her chiefly learned;
Hearts are not had as a gift but hearts are earned
By those that are not entirely beautiful;
Yet many, that have played the fool
For beauty's very self, has charm made wise,
And many a poor man that has roved,
Loved and thought himself beloved,
From a glad kindness cannot take his eyes.

May she become a flourishing hidden tree
That all her thoughts may like the linnet be,
And have no business but dispensing round
Their magnanimities of sound,
Nor but in merriment begin a chase,
Nor but in merriment a quarrel.
O may she live like some green laurel
Rooted in one dear perpetual place.

My mind, because the minds that I have loved,
The sort of beauty that I have approved,
Prosper but little, has dried up of late,
Yet knows that to be choked with hate
May well be of all evil chances chief.

If there's no hatred in a mind
Assault and battery of the wind
Can never tear the linnet from the leaf.

An intellectual hatred is the worst,
So let her think opinions are accursed.
Have I not seen the loveliest woman born
Out of the mouth of Plenty's horn,
Because of her opinionated mind
Barter that horn and every good
By quiet natures understood
For an old bellows full of angry wind?

Considering that, all hatred driven hence,
The soul recovers radical innocence
And learns at last that it is self-delighting,
Self-appeasing, self-affrighting,
And that its own sweet will is Heaven's will;
She can, though every face should scowl
And every windy quarter howl
Or every bellows burst, be happy still.

And may her bridegroom bring her to a house
Where all's accustomed, ceremonious;
For arrogance and hatred are the wares
Peddled in the thoroughfares.
How but in custom and in ceremony
Are innocence and beauty born?
Ceremony's a name for the rich horn,
And custom for the spreading laurel tree.

WILLIAM BLAKE
Infant Sorrow

My mother groand! my father wept.
Into the dangerous world I leapt:
Helpless, naked, piping loud;
Like a fiend hid in a cloud.

Struggling in my fathers hands:
Striving against my swaddling bands:
Bound and weary I thought best
To sulk upon my mothers breast.

'Let the rivers pour over my head'

———

ABSENCE AND LOSS

ADA LIMÓN
Maybe I'll Be Another Kind of Mother

Snow today, a layer outlining the maple like a halo.
or rather, a fungus. So many sharp edges·in the month.

I'm thinking I'll never sit down at the table
at the restaurant, you know that one, by the window?

Women gathered in paisley scarves with rusty iced tea,
talking about their kids, their little time-suckers,

how their mouths want so much, a gesture of exhaustion,
a roll of the eyes, *But I wouldn't have it any other way,*

their bags full of crayons and nut-free snacks, the light
coming in the window, a small tear of joy melting like ice.

No, I'll be elsewhere, having spent all day writing words
and then at the movies, where my man bought me a drink,

because our bodies are our own, and what will it be?
A blockbuster? A man somewhere saving the world, alone,

with only the thought of his family to get him through.
The film will be forgettable, a thin star in a blurred sea of
   stars,

I'll come home and rub my whole face against my dog's
belly; she'll be warm and want to sleep some more.

I'll stare at the tree and the ice will have melted, so
it's only the original tree again, green branches giving way

to other green branches, everything coming back to life.

LUCILLE CLIFTON
the lost baby poem

the time i dropped your almost body down
down to meet the waters under the city
and run one with the sewage to the sea
what did i know about waters rushing back
what did i know about drowning
or being drowned

you would have been born into winter
in the year of the disconnected gas
and no car   we would have made the thin
walk over genesee hill into the canada wind
to watch you slip like ice into strangers' hands
you would have fallen naked as snow into winter
if you were here i could tell you these
and some other things

if i am ever less than a mountain
for your definite brothers and sisters
let the rivers pour over my head
let the sea take me for a spiller
of seas   let black men call me stranger
always   for your never named sake

KAREN McCARTHY WOOLF
The Registrar's Office

isn't really an office it's a cupboard with
no source of natural light, and I don't
realise it but I'm loved up like the other
mothers gazing at meconium as if it's fresh tar
on a road not an odourless, black shit
that's been on the boil for nine months
and Lydia, that's the registrar's name, she
gives me a paper cone of iced water from
the dispenser to calm me down and it
does calm me, the water flows through
me and now we're holding each other while
Simon's down in the mortuary and I tell
her all about how he lost his mother from
a brain tumour when I was six months
gone, how her name was Lydia too, that
it was so quick and now this.
We're still holding on when he comes back
then joins us in a circle of three and even
another form to fill in can't sober me up
as the morphine unpeels another mezzanine
of hell in a shopping centre where women
with rigid quiffs and rouged cheeks glide
up and down glass escalators and
people believe in the faux marble fountains
although it's all really a shimmering
colon. Anyway, I'm determined, I say,
as I leave the room, when I get out of here, if
it's the last thing I do, I will get you
a window because that's not right, expecting

someone to live and work and sign
death certificates without a window, no-one
should have to put up with that, it's not
right, she's a good person with
a good heart, she should have a window.

ELLA WHEELER WILCOX
The Little White Hearse

Somebody's baby was buried to-day—
  The empty white hearse from the grave rumbled back,
And the morning somehow seemed less smiling and gay
  As I paused on the walk while it crossed on its way,
And a shadow seemed drawn o'er the sun's golden track.

Somebody's baby was laid out to rest,
  White as a snowdrop, and fair to behold,
And the soft little hands were crossed over the breast,
  And those hands and the lips and the eyelids were pressed
With kisses as hot as the eyelids were cold.

Somebody saw it go out of her sight,
  Under the coffin lid—out through the door;
Somebody finds only darkness and blight
  All through the glory of summer-sun light;
Somebody's baby will waken no more.

Somebody's sorrow is making me weep:
  I know not her name, but I echo her cry,
For the dearly bought baby she longed so to keep,
  The baby that rode to its long-lasting sleep
In the little white hearse that went rumbling by.

I know not her name, but her sorrow I know;
  While I paused on the crossing I lived it once more,
And back to my heart surged that river of woe
  That but in the breast of a mother can flow;
For the little white hearse has been, too, at *my* door.

BEN JONSON
On My First Son

Farewell, thou child of my right hand, and joy;
My sin was too much hope of thee, lov'd boy.
Seven years tho' wert lent to me, and I thee pay,
Exacted by thy fate, on the just day.
O, could I lose all father now! For why
Will man lament the state he should envy?
To have so soon 'scap'd world's and flesh's rage,
And if no other misery, yet age?
Rest in soft peace, and, ask'd, say, 'Here doth lie
Ben Jonson his best piece of poetry.'
For whose sake henceforth all his vows be such,
As what he loves may never like too much.

REBECCA GOSS
Her Birth

On the wall, petunias,
painted in Walberswick.
I call to you, say
That's a good omen,
that's a good sign,
before buckling,
gripping the hospital bed.

Walberswick is where
I holidayed, every childhood
summer. It's where we announced
the news. Sixteen months
after the effort of her birth,
we collect a faux-walnut
box from Jenkins & Sons.
Inside, a clear sachet,
weightless as dried herbs.

We drive two hundred
and eighty-one miles
for that cold, unstoppable
wave to suck the sachet clean
and I ask you, *She is all right now,*
isn't she? She is all right?

ROBERT HERRICK
Upon a Child That Died

Here she lies, a pretty bud,
Lately made of flesh and blood,
Who as soon fell fast asleep
As her little eyes did peep.
Give her strewings, but not stir
The earth that lightly covers her.

'A kind of faith prevails'

———

GROWING UP AND LETTING GO

FLEUR ADCOCK
For a Five-Year-Old

A snail is climbing up the window-sill
into your room, after a night of rain.
You call me in to see, and I explain
that it would be unkind to leave it there:
it might crawl to the floor; we must take care
that no one squashes it. You understand,
and carry it outside, with careful hand,
to eat a daffodil.

I see, then, that a kind of faith prevails:
your gentleness is moulded still by words
from me, who have trapped mice and shot wild birds,
from me, who drowned your kittens, who betrayed
your closest relatives, and who purveyed
the harshest kind of truth to many another.
But that is how things are: I am your mother,
and we are kind to snails.

TED HUGHES
Full Moon and Little Frieda

A cool small evening shrunk to a dog bark and the clank of a
bucket –
And you listening.
A spider's web, tense for the dew's touch.
A pail lifted, still and brimming – mirror
To tempt a first star to a tremor.

Cows are going home in the lane there, looping the hedges with
their warm wreaths of breath –
A dark river of blood, many boulders,
Balancing unspilled milk.

'Moon!' you cry suddenly, 'Moon! Moon!'

The moon has stepped back like an artist gazing amazed at a
work

That points at him amazed.

FIONA BENSON
Eurofighter Typhoon

My daughters are playing outside with plastic hoops;
the elder is trying to hula, over and over –
it falls off her hips, but she keeps trying,
and the younger is watching and giggling,
and they're happy in the bright afternoon.
I'm indoors at the hob with the door open
so I can see them, because the elder might trip,
and the younger is still a baby and liable to eat dirt,
when out of clear skies a jet comes in low
over the village. At the first muted roar
the elder runs in squealing then stops in the kitchen,
her eyes adjusting to the dimness, looking foolish
and unsure. I drop the spoon and bag of peas
and leave her frightened and tittering, wiping my hands
on my jeans, trying to walk and not run,
because I don't want to scare the baby
who's still sat on the patio alone, looking for her sister,
bewildered, trying to figure why she's gone –
all this in the odd, dead pause of the lag –
then sound catches up with the plane
and now its grey belly's right over our house
with a metallic, grinding scream
like the sky's being chainsawed open
and the baby's face drops to a square of pure fear,
she tips forward and flattens her body on the ground
and presses her face into the concrete slab.
I scoop her up and she presses in shuddering,
screaming her strange, halt pain cry
and it's all right now I tell her again and again,

69

but it's never all right now – Christ have mercy –
my daughter in my arms can't steady me –
always some woman is running to catch up her children,
we dig them out of the rubble in parts like plaster dolls –
Mary Mother of God have mercy, mercy on us all.

WENDELL BERRY
To My Children, Fearing for Them

Terrors are to come. The earth
is poisoned with narrow lives.
I think of you. What you will

live through, or perish by, eats
at my heart. What have I done? I
need better answers than there are

to the pain of coming to see
what was done in blindness,
loving what I cannot save. Nor,

your eyes turning toward me,
can I wish your lives unmade
though the pain of them is on me.

SOPHIE JEWETT
To a Child

The leaves talked in the twilight, dear;
   Hearken the tale they told:
How in some far-off place and year,
   Before the world grew old,

I was a dreaming forest tree,
   You were a wild, sweet bird
Who sheltered at the heart of me
   Because the north wind stirred;

How, when the chiding gale was still,
   When peace fell soft on fear,
You stayed one golden hour to fill
   My dream with singing, dear.

To-night the self-same songs are sung
   The first green forest heard;
My heart and the gray world grow young—
   To shelter you, my bird.

JAMES JOYCE
On the Beach at Fontana

Wind whines and whines the shingle,
The crazy pier-stakes groan;
A senile sea numbers each single
Slime-silvered stone.

From whining wind and colder
Grey sea I wrap him warm,
And touch his trembling fine-boned boyish shoulder
And trembling arm.

Around us fear, descending;
Darkness of fear above;
And in my heart how deep unending
Ache of love.

HENRY VAN DYKE
Little Boatie

a Slumber-song for the Fisherman's Child

Furl your sail, my little boatie;
    Here's the haven still and deep,
Where the dreaming tides in-streaming
    Up the channel creep.
Now the sunset breeze is dying;
Hear the plover, landward flying,
Softly down the twilight crying;
    Come to anchor, little boatie,
      In the port of Sleep.

Far away, my little boatie,
    Roaring waves are white with foam;
Ships are striving, onward driving,
    Day and night they roam.
Father's at the deep-sea trawling,
In the darkness, rowing, hauling,
While the hungry winds are calling,—
    God protect him, little boatie,
      Bring him safely home!

Not for you, my little boatie,
    Is the wide and weary sea;
You're too slender and too tender,
    You must bide with me.
All day long you have been straying
Up and down the shore and playing;

Come to harbour, no delaying!
  Day is over, little boatie,
    Night falls suddenly.

Furl your sail, my little boatie,
  Fold your wings, my weary dove.
Dews are sprinkling, stars are twinkling
  Drowsily above.
Cease from sailing, cease from rowing;
Rock upon the dream-tide, knowing
Safely o'er your rest are glowing,
  All the night, my little boatie,
    Harbour-lights of love.

GITA RALLEIGH
A Terrible Thing

Things break, beti, my little one. I'm sorry
I yelled and you cried, sorry for the shattered

snow globe, its fairytale plastic shards
and glycerine tears. But secretly I'm glad.

I've told you the stories, haven't I? On the path
to Nani's house, a sher stalks us. For each gulab

that blooms, a hundred kante prick small fingers.
Rainclouds, not sunbeams darken our garden,

a saap hisses from overgrown grass. For the bulbul
who sings sweet as you, daughter, somewhere

a pinjara swings from a balcony. Tiny nightingale
all I can do is fling the cage door wide, hope you fly.

Secretly, I'm glad you know how it is. To break
a thing and live, the thing forever broken.

beti daughter *sher* tiger *gulab* rose *kante* thorn
saap snake *bulbul* nightingale *pinjara* cage

ADRIAN MITCHELL
Beattie Is Three

At the top of the stairs
I ask for her hand. O.K.
She gives it to me.
How her fist fits my palm,
A bunch of consolation.
We take our time
Down the steep carpetway
As I wish silently
That the stairs were endless.

JACQUELINE SAPHRA
Mother. Son. Sack of Salt.

It's heavier than it looks.
but she's strong, it's nothing,

and he can help. She takes
one end, he takes the other.

Behind them they leave a trail:
there must be a hole.

Through this walking sleep
that lasts for years, the hands

of the hall clock won't be slowed,
the paintwork peels, the boy

lengthens before her eyes,
the leaking sack grows heavier.

But somewhere on the way
she knows he's taken the weight.

He's strong, he says, it's nothing.
Safe then, for her to let go.

The load is foetus-shaped,
inertly curled against his chest

but he strides forward
and away as if he's carrying

a sack of air, rounds a corner
and he's out of sight.

She hears him take the stairs
lightly, in twos, whistling.

She turns back; follows the trail
of white. She tries to gather up

everything they've left behind,
to fill her arms with salt.

RUDYARD KIPLING
If—

If you can keep your head when all about you
  Are losing theirs and blaming it on you;
If you can trust yourself when all men doubt you,
  But make allowance for their doubting too;
If you can wait and not be tired by waiting,
  Or being lied about, don't deal in lies,
Or being hated, don't give way to hating,
  And yet don't look too good, nor talk too wise:

If you can dream—and not make dreams your master;
  If you can think—and not make thoughts your aim;
If you can meet with Triumph and Disaster
  And treat those two impostors just the same;
If you can bear to hear the truth you've spoken
  Twisted by knaves to make a trap for fools,
Or watch the things you gave your life to, broken,
  And stoop and build 'em up with worn-out tools;

If you can make one heap of all your winnings
  And risk it on one turn of pitch-and-toss,
And lose, and start again at your beginnings
  And never breathe a word about your loss;
If you can force your heart and nerve and sinew
  To serve your turn long after they are gone,
And so hold on when there is nothing in you
  Except the Will which says to them: 'Hold on!'

If you can talk with crowds and keep your virtue,
  Or walk with Kings—nor lose the common touch,
If neither foes nor loving friends can hurt you,
  If all men count with you, but none too much;
If you can fill the unforgiving minute
  With sixty seconds' worth of distance run,
Yours is the Earth and everything that's in it,
  And—which is more—you'll be a Man, my son!

ELIZABETH BARRETT BROWNING
Mother and Poet

I

Dead! One of them shot by the sea in the east,
And one of them shot in the west by the sea.
Dead! both my boys! When you sit at the feast
And are wanting a great song for Italy free,
Let none look at *me*!

II

Yet I was a poetess only last year,
And good at my art, for a woman, men said;
But *this* woman, *this*, who is agonized here,
—The east sea and west sea rhyme on in her head
For ever instead.

III

What art can a woman be good at? Oh, vain!
What art *is* she good at, but hurting her breast
With the milk-teeth of babes, and a smile at the pain?
Ah boys, how you hurt! you were strong as you pressed,
And I proud, by that test.

IV

What art's for a woman? To hold on her knees
Both darlings! to feel all their arms round her throat,
Cling, strangle a little! to sew by degrees
And 'broider the long-clothes and neat little coat;
To dream and to doat.

V

To teach them . . . It stings there! *I* made them indeed
Speak plain the word *country*. I taught them, no doubt,
That a country's a thing men should die for at need.
I prated of liberty, rights, and about
The tyrant cast out.

VI

And when their eyes flashed . . . O my beautiful eyes! . . .
I exulted; nay, let them go forth at the wheels
Of the guns, and denied not. But then the surprise
When one sits quite alone! Then one weeps, then one kneels!
God, how the house feels!

VII

At first, happy news came, in gay letters moiled
With my kisses,—of camp-life and glory, and how
They both loved me; and, soon coming home to be spoiled
In return would fan off every fly from my brow
With their green laurel-bough.

VIII

Then was triumph at Turin: 'Ancona was free!'
And some one came out of the cheers in the street,
With a face pale as stone, to say something to me.
My Guido was dead! I fell down at his feet,
While they cheered in the street.

IX

I bore it; friends soothed me; my grief looked sublime
As the ransom of Italy. One boy remained
To be leant on and walked with, recalling the time
When the first grew immortal, while both of us strained
To the height he had gained.

X

And letters still came, shorter, sadder, more strong,
Writ now but in one hand, 'I was not to faint,—
One loved me for two—would be with me ere long:
And *Viva l'Italia!*—he died for, our saint,
Who forbids our complaint.'

XI

My Nanni would add, 'he was safe, and aware
Of a presence that turned off the balls,—was imprest
It was Guido himself, who knew what I could bear,
And how 'twas impossible, quite dispossessed,
To live on for the rest.'

XII

On which, without pause, up the telegraph line
Swept smoothly the next news from Gaeta:—*Shot.*
Tell his mother. Ah, ah, 'his', 'their' mother,—not 'mine',
No voice says '*My* mother' again to me. What!
You think Guido forgot?

XIII

Are souls straight so happy that, dizzy with Heaven,
They drop earth's affections, conceive not of woe?
I think not. Themselves were too lately forgiven
Through THAT Love and Sorrow which reconciled so
The Above and Below.

XIV

O Christ of the five wounds, who look'dst through the dark
To the face of Thy mother! consider, I pray,
How we common mothers stand desolate, mark,
Whose sons, not being Christs, die with eyes turned away,
And no last word to say!

XV

Both boys dead? but that's out of nature. We all
Have been patriots, yet each house must always keep one.
'Twere imbecile, hewing out roads to a wall;
And, when Italy's made, for what end is it done
If we have not a son?

XVI

Ah, ah, ah! when Gaeta's taken, what then?
When the fair wicked queen sits no more at her sport
Of the fire-balls of death crashing souls out of men?
When the guns of Cavalli with final retort
Have cut the game shore?

XVII

When Venice and Rome keep their new jubilee,
When your flag takes all heaven for its white, green, and red,
When *you* have your country from mountain to sea,
When King Victor has Italy's crown on his head,
(And *I* have my Dead)—

XVIII

What then? Do not mock me. Ah, ring your bells low,
And burn your lights faintly! *My* country is *there*,
Above the star pricked by the last peak of snow:
My Italy's THERE, with my brave civic Pair,
To disfranchise despair!

XIX

Forgive me. Some women bear children in strength,
And bite back the cry of their pain in self-scorn;
But the birth-pangs of nations will wring us at length
Into wail such as this—and we sit on forlorn
When the man-child is born.

XX

Dead! One of them shot by the sea in the east,
And one of them shot in the west by the sea.
Both! both my boys! If in keeping the feast
You want a great song for your Italy free,
Let none look at *me*!

'To thee my lay is due'

———

MOTHERS AND
MOTHER FIGURES

CHRISTINA ROSSETTI
To My Mother

To-day's your natal day;
　Sweet flowers I bring:
Mother, accept, I pray
　My offering.

And may you happy live,
　And long us bless;
Receiving as you give
　Great happiness.

LOLA RIDGE
Mother

Your love was like moonlight
turning harsh things to beauty,
so that little wry souls
reflecting each other obliquely
as in cracked mirrors . . .
beheld in your luminous spirit
their own reflection,
transfigured as in a shining stream,
and loved you for what they are not.

You are less an image in my mind
than a luster
I see you in gleams
pale as star-light on a gray wall . . .
evanescent as the reflection of a white swan
shimmering in broken water.

SUSAN MEYERS
Mother, Washing Dishes

She rarely made us do it—
we'd clear the table instead—so my sister and I teased
that some day we'd train our children right
and not end up like her, after every meal stuck
with red knuckles, a bleached rag to wipe and wring.
The one chore she spared us: gummy plates
in water greasy and swirling with sloughed peas,
globs of egg and gravy.

Or did she guard her place
at the window? Not wanting to give up the gloss
of the magnolia, the school traffic humming.
Sunset, finches at the feeder. First sightings
of the mail truck at the curb, just after noon,
delivering a note, a card, the least bit of news.

WILLIAM SHAKESPEARE
Sonnet 3

Look in thy glass and tell the face thou viewest
Now is the time that face should form another,
Whose fresh repair if now thou not renewest,
Thou dost beguile the world, unbless some mother.
For where is she so fair whose uneared womb
Disdains the tillage of thy husbandry?
Or who is he so fond will be the tomb
Of his self-love, to stop posterity?
Thou art thy mother's glass, and she in thee
Calls back the lovely April of her prime;
So thou through windows of thine age shalt see,
Despite of wrinkles, this thy golden time.
    But if thou live remembered not to be,
    Die single, and thine image dies with thee.

ROBERT LOUIS STEVENSON
To My Mother

You too, my mother, read my rhymes
For love of unforgotten times,
And you may chance to hear once more
The little feet along the floor.

LUCRETIA MARIA DAVIDSON
To My Mother

O thou whose care sustained my infant years,
    And taught my prattling lip each note of love;
Whose soothing voice breathed comfort to my fears,
    And round my brow hope's brightest garland wove;

To thee my lay is due, the simple song,
    Which Nature gave me at life's opening day;
To thee these rude, these untaught strains belong,
    Whose heart indulgent will not spurn my lay.

O say, amid this wilderness of life,
    What bosom would have throbbed like thine for me?
Who would have smiled responsive?—who in grief,
    Would e'er have felt, and, feeling, grieved like thee?

Who would have guarded, with a falcon-eye,
    Each trembling footstep or each sport of fear?
Who would have marked my bosom bounding high,
    And clasped me to her heart, with love's bright tear?

Who would have hung around my sleepless couch,
    And fanned, with anxious hand, my burning brow?
Who would have fondly pressed my fevered lip,
    In all the agony of love and wo?

None but a mother—none but one like thee,
    Whose bloom has faded in the midnight watch;
Whose eye, for me, has lost its witchery,
    Whose form has felt disease's mildew touch.

Yes, thou hast lighted me to health and life,
    By the bright lustre of thy youthful bloom—
Yes, thou hast wept so oft o'er every grief,
    That wo hath traced thy brow with marks of gloom.

O then, to thee, this rude and simple song,
    Which breathes of thankfulness and love for thee,
To thee, my mother, shall this lay belong,
    Whose life is spent in toil and care for me.

EDGAR ALLAN POE
To My Mother

Because I feel that, in the Heavens above,
The angels, whispering to one another,
Can find, among their burning terms of love,
None so devotional as that of 'Mother',
Therefore by that dear name I long have called you—
You who are more than mother unto me,
And fill my heart of hearts, where Death installed you
In setting my Virginia's spirit free.
My mother—my own mother, who died early,
Was but the mother of myself; but you
Are mother to the one I loved so dearly,
And thus are dearer than the mother I knew
By that infinity with which my wife
Was dearer to my soul than its soul-life.

SELIMA HILL
Mother Stone

My father was a tall man who approved of beating,
but my mother, like a mother stone,
preferred us to be sitting in a small room
lined with damson-coloured velvet
thinking quietly to ourselves, undisturbed;
everything was slow and beautiful
when we were being punished: all we had to do
was watch the dark-red petals' roses
press against each other in a slight breeze
on the window pane, and blossoms fall
in silence from the cherry-tree;

and now my son is lying in a long white shirt
across our eiderdown, trying to stay awake,
and fingering my spine's shell pink as if I was a beach
and he was blades of marram grass in drifts of sand.
I dab my face with cream that smells of cucumber
and whisper in a distant milky voice
Of course I'll wake you up when he comes;
and then his eyelids close,
and in his self-created darkness he is following
a big car on a motorway at night,
it turns into the driveway to the house,
and presently the driver gets out:
it is only a bear in the moonlight,
walking on the lavender beds.

MATTHEW SIEGEL
Matthew you're leaving again so soon

please take these pens I have all these pens
for you all with caps on them and pen holders
I have all these pen holders large and plastic

I know they won't fit in your bag I'll mail them
take this umbrella this sweater these socks
they're ankle length like you like them

and soup take this soup I froze four batches
in Tupperware four batches of broth and chicken
and carrots and celery frozen in the freezer

they will keep you healthy my son
my liver take my liver to help clean your blood
I'll fly to you I'll come to you tomorrow

you used to cling to my ankle and I would
drag you across the floor please
pack me in your suitcase take me with you

MARY JEAN CHAN
postscript

in the penultimate scene where mother
and child are listening to one another

speak in spite of everything the way
an orchestra might play on bravely

even when the audience claps before
it's time you will want to stay awhile

in subtropical winter heat as sunlight
blazes through the fog of memory you

begin to wonder if the origin story can
at last be transfigured into the version

redacted through the centuries (the one
in which the garden comes alive) a queer

child's vision of paradise where the trees
are free to bear their multitudinous light

PHILIP LARKIN
Mother, Summer, I

My mother, who hates thunderstorms,
Holds up each summer day and shakes
It out suspiciously, lest swarms
Of grape-dark clouds are lurking there;
But when the August weather breaks
And rains begin, and brittle frost
Sharpens the bird-abandoned air,
Her worried summer look is lost.

And I her son, though summer-born
And summer-loving, none the less
Am easier when the leaves are gone;
Too often summer days appear
Emblems of perfect happiness
I can't confront: I must await
A time less bold, less rich, less clear:
An autumn more appropriate.

'Only a dad with a tired face'

———

FATHERS AND
FATHER FIGURES

WILLIAM WORDSWORTH
My heart leaps up when I behold

My heart leaps up when I behold
   A rainbow in the sky:
So was it when my life began;
So is it now I am a man;
So be it when I shall grow old,
   Or let me die!
The Child is father of the Man;
And I could wish my days to be
Bound each to each by natural piety.

EDGAR GUEST
Only a Dad

Only a dad with a tired face,
Coming home from the daily race,
Bringing little of gold or fame
To show how well he has played the game;
But glad in his heart that his own rejoice
To see him come and to hear his voice.

Only a dad with a brood of four,
One of ten million men or more
Plodding along in the daily strife,
Bearing the whips and the scorns of life,
With never a whimper of pain or hate,
For the sake of those who at home await.

Only a dad, neither rich nor proud,
Merely one of the surging crowd
Toiling, striving from day to day,
Facing whatever may come his way,
Silent whenever the harsh condemn,
And bearing it all for the love of them.

Only a dad but he gives his all
To smooth the way for his children small,
Doing with courage stern and grim,
The deeds that his father did for him.
This is the line that for him I pen:
Only a dad, but the best of men.

NAOMI SHIHAB NYE
My Father and the Figtree

For other fruits my father was indifferent.
He'd point at the cherry trees and say,
'See those? I wish they were figs.'
In the evenings he sat by my bed
weaving folktales like vivid little scarves.
They always involved a figtree.
Even when it didn't fit, he'd stick it in.
Once Joha was walking down the road and he saw a figtree.
Or, he tied his camel to a figtree and went to sleep.
Or, later when they caught and arrested him,
his pockets were full of figs.

At age six I ate a dried fig and shrugged.
'That's not what I'm talking about!' he said,
'I'm talking about a fig straight from the earth—
gift of Allah!—on a branch so heavy it touches the ground.
I'm talking about picking the largest fattest sweetest fig
in the world and putting it in my mouth.'
(Here he'd stop and close his eyes.)

Years passed, we lived in many houses, none had figtrees.
We had lima beans, zucchini, parsley, beets.
'Plant one!' my mother said, but my father never did.
He tended garden half-heartedly, forgot to water,
let the okra get too big.
'What a dreamer he is. Look how many things he starts
and doesn't finish.'

The last time he moved, I got a phone call.
My father, in Arabic, chanting a song I'd never heard.
'What's that?'
'Wait till you see!'
He took me out to the new yard.
There, in the middle of Dallas, Texas,
a tree with the largest, fattest, sweetest figs in the world.
'It's a figtree song!' he said,
plucking his fruits like ripe tokens,
emblems, assurance
of a world that was always his own.

ANNE BRADSTREET
To Her Father with Some Verses

Most truly honoured, and as truly dear,
If worth in me or ought I do appear,
Who can of right better demand the same
Than may your worthy self from whom it came?
The principal might yield a greater sum,
Yet handled ill, amounts but to this crumb;
My stock's so small I know not how to pay,
My bond remains in force unto this day;
Yet for part payment take this simple mite,
Where nothing's to be had, kings loose their right.
Such is my debt I may not say forgive,
But as I can, I'll pay it while I live;
Such is my bond, none can discharge but I,
Yet paying is not paid until I die.

WILFRED OWEN
The Parable of the Old Man and the Young

So Abram rose, and clave the wood, and went,
And took the fire with him, and a knife.
And as they sojourned both of them together,
Isaac the first-born spake and said, My Father,
Behold the preparations, fire and iron,
But where the lamb, for this burnt-offering?
Then Abram bound the youth with belts and straps,
And builded parapets and trenches there,
And stretched forth the knife to slay his son.
When lo! an Angel called him out of heaven,
Saying, Lay not thy hand upon the lad,
Neither do anything to him, thy son.
Behold! Caught in a thicket by its horns,
A Ram. Offer the Ram of Pride instead.

But the old man would not so, but slew his son,
And half the seed of Europe, one by one.

LI-YOUNG LEE
The Gift

To pull the metal splinter from my palm
my father recited a story in a low voice.
I watched his lovely face and not the blade.
Before the story ended, he'd removed
the iron sliver I thought I'd die from.

I can't remember the tale,
but hear his voice still, a well
of dark water, a prayer.
And I recall his hands,
two measures of tenderness
he laid against my face,
the flames of discipline
he raised above my head.

Had you entered that afternoon
you would have thought you saw a man
planting something in a boy's palm,
a silver tear, a tiny flame.
Had you followed that boy
you would have arrived here,
where I bend over my wife's right hand.

Look how I shave her thumbnail down
so carefully she feels no pain.
Watch as I lift the splinter out.
I was seven when my father
took my hand like this,
and I did not hold that shard

between my fingers and think,
Metal that will bury me,
christen it Little Assassin,
Ore Going Deep for My Heart.

And I did not lift up my wound and cry,
Death visited here!
I did what a child does
when he's given something to keep.
I kissed my father.

HOMER
from *The Odyssey*

translated by Alexander Pope

'Few are my days (Ulysses made reply),
Nor I, alas! descendant of the sky.
I am thy father. O my son! my son!
That father, for whose sake thy days have run
One scene of woe! to endless cares consign'd,
And outraged by the wrongs of base mankind.'

Then, rushing to his arms, he kiss'd his boy
With the strong raptures of a parent's joy.
Tears bathe his cheek, and tears the ground bedew:
He strain'd him close, as to his breast he grew.
'Ah me! (exclaims the prince with fond desire)
Thou art not—no, thou canst not be my sire.
Heaven such illusion only can impose,
By the false joy to aggravate my woes.
Who but a god can change the general doom,
And give to wither'd age a youthful bloom!
Late, worn with years, in weeds obscene you trod;
Now, clothed in majesty, you move a god!'

'Forbear (he cried,) for Heaven reserve that name;
Give to thy father but a father's claim;
Other Ulysses shalt thou never see,
I am Ulysses, I, my son, am he.
Twice ten sad years o'er earth and ocean toss'd,
'Tis given at length to view my native coast.
Pallas, unconquer'd maid, my frame surrounds

With grace divine: her power admits no bounds;
She o'er my limbs old age and wrinkles shed;
Now strong as youth, magnificent I tread.
The gods with ease frail man depress or raise,
Exalt the lowly, or the proud debase.'

He spoke and sate. The prince with transport flew,
Hung round his neck, while tears his cheek bedew;
Nor less the father pour'd a social flood;
They wept abundant, and they wept aloud.
As the bold eagle with fierce sorrow stung,
Or parent vulture, mourns her ravish'd young;
They cry, they scream, their unfledged brood a prey
To some rude churl, and borne by stealth away:
So they aloud: and tears in tides had run,
Their grief unfinish'd with the setting sun;
But checking the full torrent in its flow,
The prince thus interrupts the solemn woe.
'What ship transported thee, O father, say;
And what bless'd hands have oar'd thee on the way?'

'All, all (Ulysses instant made reply),
I tell thee all, my child, my only joy!'

ROBINSON JEFFERS
To His Father

Christ was your lord and captain all your life,
He fails the world but you he did not fail,
He led you through all forms of grief and strife
Intact, a man full-armed, he let prevail
Nor outward malice nor the worse-fanged snake
That coils in one's own brain against your calm,
That great rich jewel well guarded for his sake
With coronal age and death like quieting balm.
I Father having followed other guides
And oftener to my hurt no leader at all,
Through years nailed up like dripping panther hides
For trophies on a savage temple wall
Hardly anticipate that reverend stage
Of life, the snow-wreathed honor of extreme age.

ROBERT HAYDEN
Those Winter Sundays

Sundays too my father got up early
and put his clothes on in the blueblack cold,
then with cracked hands that ached
from labor in the weekday weather made
banked fires blaze. No one ever thanked him.

I'd wake and hear the cold splintering, breaking.
When the rooms were warm, he'd call,
and slowly I would rise and dress,
fearing the chronic angers of that house,

Speaking indifferently to him,
who had driven out the cold
and polished my good shoes as well.
What did I know, what did I know
of love's austere and lonely offices?

ROGER ROBINSON
Sleep

It becomes clear to you
the night your father asks you
to wake him up to see
his favourite film on TV,
and despite cups of coffee
bright lights and company
he is asleep
with his dark rimmed glasses
tilted on his face
before the opening credits.

And there
hearing the drag of his snore
and watching the uncomfortably
crooked angle of his neck,
you see him at nineteen,
taking care of his four brothers
and one sister and studying
for a scholarship while working
nights pushing dead bodies
at the local morgue, and he's tired
but he can't stop because he'll
be the first in their family
to go to university and he can't let them down.

At twenty-one
he's in class at Stirling University
wondering if he can afford the batteries
for his warehouseman's torch

so he can study on the job tonight.
Nobody told him Scotland
would be this cold, and it's
so lonely sometimes but he
has to pass these exams
or he'll be out.

At twenty-two you're born.
Your mother works the night shift
at the hospital, and he tries to read
between your two a.m. squeals
and he picks you up
in the hand not holding the book
and smiles and rocks you to sleep.

Twenty-five now,
and working late five nights a week
trying to snatch a few promotions,
and somehow he thought
it might be a bit easier with his degree,
and he really needs
to move his wife and kids
into a place of their own.

And for the next twenty years
he battles on his job every day
just so you could be comfortable
and have the space to be what you want.

And then you know
that he's never had much time for this
for rest, for sleep.
You prop his head with a pillow,

gingerly pull off his glasses
and stare at him
snoring, loudly,
beautifully.

*'We her children hold on like
drought holds out for rain'*

———————

CHANGE AND AGEING

MALIKA BOOKER
The Little Miracles

after 'A Winter Night' by Tomas Tranströmer
translated by Robin Robertson

Since I found mother collapsed on the kitchen
floor, we siblings have become blindfolded mules

harnessed to carts filled with strain, lumbering
through a relentless storm, wanting to make

our mother walk on her own again, wanting to rest
our palms on her left leg and arm like Jesus, but

constellations do not gather like leaves in a teacup,
so what miracle, of what blood, of what feeble wishes

do we pray, happy no nails hammer plywood, building
a coffin, to house her dead weight, happy her journey

crawls as we her children hold on like drought holds out
for rain, learning what it is like to begin again, start

with the, the, the dog, the cat, the date, the year, the
stroke, the brain, the fenced in walls, she struggles

to dismantle brick on brick. *She cannot break this,*
we reason, watching her left hand in her lap, a useless

echo. We chew bitter bush, swallow our howling storm,
reluctantly splintering under the strain of our mother's

ailing bed-rest. We smile at each of her feats: right hand
brushing her teeth in late evening, head able to lift

without the aid of a neck-brace, her offspring's names
Malika, Phillip and Kwesi are chants repeated over

and over as if staking us children as her life's work,
her blessings, showing how much we are loved. The days

she sings *walk with me oh my Lord*, over and over, *walk
with me oh my Lord, through the darkest night* . . . and I sing

with her, my tones flat to her soprano, *just as you changed
the wind and walked upon the sea, conquer, my living Lord,*

the storm that threatens me, and we sing and sing until
she says, *Maliks, please stop the cat-wailing before*

*you voice mek rain fall, and look how the weather nice
outside eh!* Then we laugh and laugh until almost giddy,

our mood light momentarily in this sterile room, where
each spoonful of pureed food slipped into her mouth

like a tender offering takes us a step away from feeding
tubes, and we are so thankful for each minuscule miracle.

ALISON BINNEY
Muscle Memory

Three weeks earlier I'd said *My Dad has Alzheimer's*
to the sashed woman in the porch who swept me
past the kiosk through the transept to the vestry.
The first time I'd said it aloud: I sounded older,
as if I knew just what you needed and how to find it.
She offered me up to the vergers – *This lady is enquiring*
about Christmas Eve. Her father has Alzheimer's –
who tumbled over themselves to show how welcome you'd be,
dementia and all, while I stood like a lost child in a shop.

So, at the end of the year of lost things, we came here,
to sit by the copper font that stretched our faces like toffee,
where giant candelabra breathed wax down the nave,
and the cathedral cat slipped between chairs and feet
to bag a warm vent. And where, when the organ rumbled
the chords of *Hark the Herald*, you pushed yourself up
on the frame to stand straight-backed, singing the bass line
by heart while the great west door swung open.

WAYNE HOLLOWAY-SMITH
The posh mums are boxing in the square

roughing each other up   in a nice way
This is not the world into which I was born
        so I'm changing it
I'm sinking deep into the past and dressing my own mum
in their blue spandexes
svelte black stripes from hip to hem
and husbands with better dispositions toward kindness
or at least   I'm giving her new lungs
I'm giving her a best friend   with no problems and both of
    them pads
some gloves to go at each other with   in a nice way
I'm making it a warm day for them but also
I'm making it rain
the two of them dapping it out in long shadows
I'm watching her from the trees grow
strength in her thighs   my mum
grow strength in her glutes my mum
her back taught upright
her knees
and watching her grow no bad thing in her stomach no
    tumour
her feet do not hurt to touch   my mum she is hopping
sinews are happening
wiry arms developing their full reach
no bad thing explodes

sweat and not gradual death   I'm cheering
no thing in her stomach no alcohol
no cigarettes with their crotonaldehyde let my dad keep those

no removal of her womb
– and I'm cheering her on in better condition
cheering she is learning to fight for her own body
in spandex her new life
and though there is no beef between them
if her friend is gaining the upper hand
I will call out from the trees
       her name
              Christine!
and when she turns   as turn she must
my mum   in the nicest possible way
can slug her right in the gut

SEAMUS HEANEY
The Butts

His suits hung in the wardrobe, broad
And short
And slightly bandy-sleeved,

Flattened back
Against themselves,
A bit stand-offish.

Stale smoke and oxter-sweat
Came at you in a stirred-up brew
When you reached in,

A whole rake of thornproof and blue serge
Swung heavily
Like waterweed disturbed. I sniffed

Tonic unfreshness,
Then delved past flap and lining
For the forbidden handfuls.

But a kind of empty-handedness
Transpired . . . Out of suit-cloth
Pressed against my face,

Out of those layered stuffs
That surged and gave,
Out of the cold smooth pocket-lining

Nothing but chaff cocoons,
A paperiness not known again
Until the last days came

And we must learn to reach well in beneath
Each meagre armpit
To lift and sponge him,

One on either side,
Feeling his lightness,
Having to dab and work

Closer than anybody liked
But having, for all that,
To keep working.

RUTH FAINLIGHT
Handbag

My mother's old leather handbag,
crowded with letters she carried
all through the war. The smell
of my mother's handbag: mints
and lipstick and Coty powder.
The look of those letters, softened
and worn at the edges, opened,
read, and refolded so often.
Letters from my father. Odour
of leather and powder, which ever
since then has meant womanliness,
and love, and anguish, and war.

RON CAREY
Upstairs

Lying on the bed with my mother,
Wearing my father's Alpaca overcoat.
Here, Upstairs, where the air is old
And the blue-painted radiators are singing
And the cold cream is liquefying on the dressing table.
My mother can no longer take the cold.

My father was my age when he died.
I look like him everyone says I look SO like him everyone says.
I had to think when she asked me to wear the coat,
For a moment I had to think about it like I didn't know what
    she meant.
It was then she called me Danny too many times Danny she
    called me.
Please, Danny, she said.
So I put on the coat.

She wants to lie down the pain for a moment, just for a
    moment,
On to the pink candlewick spread, Upstairs, where her body
    will not take her.
So I lift her in my arms. So light. Oh! Sarah you are SO
    light. I carry her.
Up. To the age before one is old.
Up where Sarah and Danny once moved in the fluid
Of young bodies and slept, hot to the touch.

We pretend to sleep, Danny and me,
Though I sweat in the coat and I don't feel well.
But I stay still, for Sarah's sake I am still.
The afternoon seagulls are mad at something in the garden.
I should investigate because they sound so near and real
    and mad but I can't
Because she will not let go of his hand.

After a while, released into the darkness, I get up.
I see very little by the nibbling light of the Sacred Heart.
Sarah. Softly.
Sarah. Quietly.
Sarah. My father's voice.
And she says nothing she says, nothing.
Leaving me, afraid
That everything might be said and done and said
And she has taken all the cold of the earth into herself.

KAYO CHINGONYI
Kumukanda

Since I haven't danced among my fellow initiates,
following a looped procession from woods at the edge
of a village, Tata's people would think me unfinished –
a child who never sloughed off the childish estate
to cross the river boys of our tribe must cross
in order to die and come back grown.

I was raised in a strange land, by small increments:
when I bathed my mother the days she was too weak,
when auntie broke the news and I chose a yellow suit
and white shoes to dress my mother's body,
at the grave-side when the man I almost grew to call
dad, though we both needed a hug, shook my hand.

If my alternate self, who never left, could see me
what would he make of these literary pretensions,
this need to speak with a tongue that isn't mine?
Would he be strange to me as I to him, frowning
as he greets me in the language of my father
and my father's father and my father's father's father?

'& the whole garden will bow'

FAREWELLS AND RENEWAL

e. e. cummings
from *Portraits*

2

if there are any heavens my mother will(all by herself)have
one.   It will not be a pansy heaven nor
a fragile heaven of lilies-of-the-valley but
it will be a heaven of blackred roses

my father will be(deep like a rose
tall like a rose)

standing near my

swaying over her
(silent)
with eyes which are really petals and see

nothing with the face of a poet really which
is a flower and not a face with
hands
which whisper
This is my beloved my

                        (suddenly in sunlight
he will bow,

& the whole garden will bow)

TONY HARRISON
Book Ends

I

Baked the day she suddenly dropped dead
we chew it slowly that last apple pie.

Shocked into sleeplessness you're scared of bed.
We never could talk much, and now don't try.

You're like book ends, the pair of you, she'd say,
Hog that grate, say nothing, sit, sleep, stare . . .

The 'scholar' me, you, worn out on poor pay,
only our silence made us seem a pair.

Not as good for staring in, blue gas,
too regular each bud, each yellow spike.

A night you need my company to pass
and she not here to tell us we're alike!

Your life's all shattered into smithereens.

Back in our silences and sullen looks,
for all the Scotch we drink, what's still between 's
not the thirty or so years, but books, books, books.

II

The stone's too full. The wording must be terse.
There's scarcely room to carve the FLORENCE on it –

Come on, it's not as if we're wanting verse.
It's not as if we're wanting a whole sonnet!

After tumblers of neat *Johnny Walker*
(I think that both of us we're on our third)
you said you'd always been a clumsy talker
and couldn't find another, shorter word
for 'beloved' or for 'wife' in the inscription,
but not too clumsy that you can't still cut:

You're supposed to be the bright boy at description
and you can't tell them what the fuck to put!

I've got to find the right words on my own.

I've got the envelope that he'd been scrawling,
mis-spelt, mawkish, stylistically appalling
but I can't squeeze more love into their stone.

OCEAN VUONG
Telemachus

Like any good son, I pull my father out
of the water, drag him by his hair

through white sand, his knuckles carving a trail
the waves rush in to erase. Because the city

beyond the shore is no longer
where we left it. Because the bombed

cathedral is now a cathedral
of trees. I kneel beside him to see how far

I might sink. *Do you know who I am,
Ba?* But the answer never comes. The answer

is the bullet hole in his back, brimming
with seawater. He is so still I think

he could be anyone's father, found
the way a green bottle might appear

at a boy's feet containing a year
he has never touched. I touch

his ears. No use. I turn him
over. To face it. The cathedral

in his sea-black eyes. The face
not mine – but one I will wear

to kiss all my lovers good-night:
the way I seal my father's lips

with my own & begin
the faithful work of drowning.

LORNA GOODISON
My Mother's Sea Chanty

I dream that I am washing
my mother's body in the night sea
and that she sings slow
and that she still breathes.

I see my sweet mother
a plump mermaid in my dreams
and I wash her white hair
with ambergris and foaming seaweed.

I watch my mother under water
gather the loose pearls she finds,
scrub them free from nacre
and string them on a lost fishing line.

I hear my dark mother
speaking sea-speak with pilot fish,
showing them how to direct barks
that bear away our grief.

I pray my mother breaks free
from the fish pots and marine chores
of her residence beneath the sea,
and that she rides a wild white horse.

FAWZIA MURADALI KANE
Washing the Body

I was the coward. The others were calm. They knew what they had to do. Our cousin Zen was there, she had done this before. Zen is a happy person. She made us giggle in the waiting room, while the funeral director was telling us everybody have a sense they will pass about say maybe forty days before. Even if they go by accident, he said, and if you see somebody talking to the dead like normal, then you know it ain't going to be long now. Our mother had lain on her sickbed, calling out for us to open the gate for my uncle and them to come in. They outside waiting by the gate, she cried, they in traffic jam, they need to free up. That uncle had died twenty years before. Zen said to the funeral man, eh heh? well that is a nice and cheerful thought! We had to walk past the showroom – elaborate decorated trays to choose one from, the man said, as Muslims don't need coffins, only rattan baskets to degrade quick, dust to dust and thing. He was kind, in his way. Used to the need for speed of these burials. A lady led us into the washing room for the ritual to start. She went into the walk-in fridge and pulled Mammy out on a trolley, wrapped in her bedsheet. oh gorsh she stiff, big sister said, it don't look like she. The lady talked us through the stages, how to wash, how to keep the parts covered to preserve modesty. What prayers to say. She handed out new rubber gloves and showed us the hose spray head. Middle sister unwrapped the bedsheet from Mammy slow and careful and then we all didn't, couldn't move. Then youngest sister steups and said, all you stop this stupidness okay this is not her okay this is just a shell. She snapped on the gloves and held her hands up like a surgeon and said let's get to work. Brisk brisk just like so. And then and there we saw the fifteen years of her A&E nursing, the calm assessment of disaster with its triage of the distraught, not the images of our forever youngest etched in our minds, the toddler dancing in nappies, or hearing the teenager arguing in the porch with Mammy who would be sobbing: don't ever say I don't love you, you the last one, you go always be my baby!

ELIZABETH AKERS ALLEN
Rock Me to Sleep

Backward, turn backward, O Time, in your flight,
Make me a child again just for tonight!
Mother, come back from the echoless shore,
Take me again to your heart as of yore;
Kiss from my forehead the furrows of care,
Smooth the few silver threads out of my hair;
Over my slumbers your loving watch keep; –
Rock me to sleep, mother, – rock me to sleep!

Backward, flow backward, O tide of the years!
I am so weary of toil and of tears, –
Toil without recompense, tears all in vain, –
Take them, and give me my childhood again!
I have grown weary of dust and decay, –
Weary of flinging my soul-wealth away;
Weary of sowing for others to reap; –
Rock me to sleep, mother – rock me to sleep!

Tired of the hollow, the base, the untrue,
Mother, O mother, my heart calls for you!
Many a summer the grass has grown green,
Blossomed and faded, our faces between:
Yet, with strong yearning and passionate pain,
Long I tonight for your presence again.
Come from the silence so long and so deep; –
Rock me to sleep, mother, – rock me to sleep!

Over my heart, in the days that are flown,
No love like mother-love ever has shone;
No other worship abides and endures, –
Faithful, unselfish, and patient like yours:
None like a mother can charm away pain
From the sick soul and the world-weary brain.
Slumber's soft calms o'er my heavy lids creep; –
Rock me to sleep, mother, – rock me to sleep!

Come, let your brown hair, just lighted with gold,
Fall on your shoulders again as of old;
Let it drop over my forehead tonight,
Shading my faint eyes away from the light;
For with its sunny-edged shadows once more
Haply will throng the sweet visions of yore;
Lovingly, softly, its bright billows sweep; –
Rock me to sleep, mother, – rock me to sleep!

Mother, dear mother, the years have been long
Since I last listened your lullaby song:
Sing, then, and unto my soul it shall seem
Womanhood's years have been only a dream.
Clasped to your heart in a loving embrace,
With your light lashes just sweeping my face,
Never hereafter to wake or to weep; –
Rock me to sleep, mother, – rock me to sleep!

D. H. LAWRENCE
Piano

Softly, in the dusk, a woman is singing to me;
Taking me back down the vista of years, till I see
A child sitting under the piano, in the boom of the tingling
strings
And pressing the small, poised feet of a mother who smiles
as she sings.

In spite of myself, the insidious mastery of song
Betrays me back, till the heart of me weeps to belong
To the old Sunday evenings at home, with winter outside
And hymns in the cosy parlour, the tinkling piano our guide.

So now it is vain for the singer to burst into clamour
With the great black piano appassionato. The glamour
Of childish days is upon me, my manhood is cast
Down in the flood of remembrance, I weep like a child for
the past.

ANNE CARSON
Father's Old Blue Cardigan

Now it hangs on the back of the kitchen chair
where I always sit, as it did
on the back of the kitchen chair where he always sat.

I put it on whenever I come in,
as he did, stamping
the snow from his boots.

I put it on and sit in the dark.
He would not have done this.
Coldness comes paring down from the moonbone in
    the sky.

His laws were a secret.
But I remember the moment at which I knew
he was going mad inside his laws.

He was standing at the turn of the driveway when
    I arrived.
He had on the blue cardigan with the buttons done up
    all the way to the top.
Not only because it was a hot July afternoon

but the look on his face—
as a small child who has been dressed by some aunt early
    in the morning
for a long trip

on cold trains and windy platforms
will sit very straight at the edge of his seat
while the shadows like long fingers

over the haystacks that sweep past
keep shocking him
because he is riding backwards.

ANNE SEXTON
All My Pretty Ones

Father, this year's jinx rides us apart
where you followed our mother to her cold slumber;
a second shock boiling its stone to your heart,
leaving me here to shuffle and disencumber
you from the residence you could not afford:
a gold key, your half of a woolen mill,
twenty suits from Dunne's, an English Ford,
the love and legal verbiage of another will,
boxes of pictures of people I do not know.
I touch their cardboard faces. They must go.

But the eyes, as thick as wood in this album,
hold me. I stop here, where a small boy
waits in a ruffled dress for someone to come . . .
for this soldier who holds his bugle like a toy
or for this velvet lady who cannot smile.
Is this your father's father, this commodore
in a mailman suit? My father, time meanwhile
has made it unimportant who you are looking for.
I'll never know what these faces are all about.
I lock them into their book and throw them out.

This is the yellow scrapbook that you began
the year I was born; as crackling now and wrinkly
as tobacco leaves: clippings where Hoover outran
the Democrats, wiggling his dry finger at me
and Prohibition; news where the *Hindenburg* went
down and recent years where you went flush
on war. This year, solvent but sick, you meant

to marry that pretty widow in a one-month rush.
But before you had that second chance, I cried
on your fat shoulder. Three days later you died.

These are the snapshots of marriage, stopped in places.
Side by side at the rail toward Nassau now;
here, with the winner's cup at the speedboat races,
here, in tails at the Cotillion, you take a bow,
here, by our kennel of dogs with their pink eyes,
running like show-bred pigs in their chain-link pen;
here, at the horseshow where my sister wins a prize;
and here, standing like a duke among groups of men.
Now I fold you down, my drunkard, my navigator,
my first lost keeper, to love or look at later.

I hold a five-year diary that my mother kept
for three years, telling all she does not say
of your alcoholic tendency. You overslept,
she writes. My God, father, each Christmas Day
with your blood, will I drink down your glass
of wine? The diary of your hurly-burly years
goes to my shelf to wait for my age to pass.
Only in this hoarded span will love persevere.
Whether you are pretty or not, I outlive you,
bend down my strange face to yours and forgive you.

HARTLEY COLERIDGE
Lines—

I have been cherish'd and forgiven
    By many tender-hearted,
'Twas for the sake of one in Heaven
    Of *him* that is departed.

Because I bear my Father's name
    I am not quite despised,
My little legacy of fame
    I've not yet realized.

And yet if you should praise myself
    I'll tell you, I had rather
You'd give your love to me, poor elf,
    Your praise to my great father.

JESSIE B. RITTENHOUSE
My Father

My father was a tall man and yet the ripened rye
Would come above his shoulders, the spears shot up so high.

My father was a tall man and yet the tasseled corn
Would hide him when he cut the stalks upon a frosty morn.

The green things grew so lushly in the valley of my birth,
Where else could one witness the luxuriance of earth?

The plow would turn so rhythmically the loose, unfettered loam,
There was no need of effort to drive the coulter home.

My father walked behind his team before the sun was high,
Fine as a figure on a frieze cut sharp against the sky.

And when he swung the cradle in the yellow of the grain,
He could command all eyes around, or when he drove the wain.

I wonder if his acres now that lie so far away
Are waiting for his footprint at the coming of the day.

I wonder if the brown old barn that still is standing long
And ghostly cattle in the stalls are waiting for his song.

EMILY BERRY
Canopy

The weather was inside.

The branches trembled over the glass as if to apologise; then they thumped and they came in.

And the trees shook everything off until they were bare and clean. They held on to the ground with their long feet and leant into the gale and back again.

This was their way with the wind.

They flung us down and flailed above us with their visions and their pale tree light.

I think they were telling us to survive. That's what a leaf feels like anyway. We lay under their great awry display and they tattooed us with light.

They got inside us and made us speak; I said my first word in their language: 'canopy'.

I was crying and it felt like I was feeding. Be my mother, I said to the trees, in the language of trees, which can't be transcribed, and they shook their hair back, and they bent low with their many arms, and they looked into my eyes as only trees can look into the eyes of a person, they touched me with the rain on their fingers till I was all droplets, till I was a mist, and they said they would.

THOMAS HARDY
Heredity

I am the family face;
Flesh perishes, I live on,
Projecting trait and trace
Through time to times anon,
And leaping from place to place
Over oblivion.

The years-heired feature that can
In curve and voice and eye
Despise the human span
Of durance – that is I;
The eternal thing in man,
That heeds no call to die.

AFTERWORD

Our families will probably bring us the most joy in life – and probably the most sorrow. Poets tend to home in on high emotion for their subject matter, so it shouldn't come as a surprise that they have been writing about the elation and the heartbreak we associate with our loved ones since the very beginning. They are there in *Gilgamesh* and *The Odyssey*, and in the most recent work of our contemporary poets. Poetic styles might have changed but the practice of parents writing poems about their children and children writing poems about their parents has remained constant for thousands of years. The theme seems inexhaustible; relationships of this kind are eternally familiar yet endlessly unfathomable.

From the beginning of my writing life, I composed poems about my parents, probably taking my cue from Tony Harrison's astonishingly honest and relatable pieces about his mother and father, and from Robert Lowell's family and domestic poems. As truculent and argumentative as I could be at times, I never wanted to judge my parents in my work, as Larkin seems to in his famously sweary poem 'This Be The Verse'. My dad became a great friend, maybe my best friend, and my poems about him were always explorations of that relationship. For some reason, they often had a slightly elegiac or commemorative tone, even when he was very much alive and kicking – preparation work of some kind, perhaps. When he died, it took a long while for me to accept that I would never talk to him again, and when at last poems of bereavement and loss started to emerge, they were attempts at a conversation, no matter how one-sided. My mum has been harder to write about; in comparison to my dad, everyone is quieter and subtler and more difficult to characterise. But she's there in the poems as a gracious and caring presence, I hope – a working mother with all the dignity and difficulties that come with the job.

When I had a daughter, I imagined that my poetic perspective would shift towards her, and that psychologically I would pivot from the role of son to the role of father. But, except indirectly, she's largely absent from my work. To some degree, I've always been conscious of respecting her privacy and not trying to fix her identity in metaphors and half-rhymes. It's what all poets who write about their nearest and dearest must ask themselves: do I have the right? What will the consequences be? Besides which, my daughter was forced to study my work in school, and I assumed that she'd have had enough poems to deal with in her life without *being* one. Parents are a puzzle but children are a complete mystery – half kin, half strangers – and perhaps any attempt to capture her in words has always been beyond me.

The Thomas Hardy poem 'Heredity' that closes this collection reads as a cold-eyed observation which is also a testament to the involuntary bond between ancestors and dependants, spoken not by a person but by the physical features passed down from one generation to the next. It makes an intriguing counterpart to the opening poem, Maura Dooley's 'Freight', a hopeful and doting poem addressed to a baby in the womb 'whose history's already charted / in a rope of cells'. Throughout this anthology, all the poems seem to find a position on a sliding scale between science and love. Compelled, captivated, mesmerised and bemused (and occasionally repulsed), poets have always written about the ties that bind, and they always will.

SIMON ARMITAGE, 2026

158

ACKNOWLEDGEMENTS

We are grateful to the following for permission to reproduce copyright material:

MAURA DOOLEY: 'Freight' from *Sound Barrier: Poems 1982–2002*, Bloodaxe Books, 2002. Reproduced by permission of Bloodaxe Books, www.bloodaxebooks.com

CAROLINE BIRD: 'Primitive Heart' from *The Air Year*, Carcanet, 2020. Reproduced by permission of Carcanet Press Limited

GAIL McCONNELL: 'Orange' from *Fothermather*, copyright © Gail McConnell, 2019. Reproduced by permission of Ink Sweat & Tears Press

JAN-HENRY GRAY: 'April 1984' from *Documents*, copyright © Jan-Henry Gray, 2019. Reproduced by permission of The Permissions Company, LLC on behalf of BOA Editions, Ltd, boaeditions.org

ANNE STEVENSON: 'Poem for a Daughter' from *Collected Poems*, Bloodaxe Books, 2023. Reproduced by permission of Bloodaxe Books, www.bloodaxebooks.com

RACHEL RICHARDSON: 'Shearwater' from *Hundred-Year Wave*, copyright © Rachel Richardson, 2016. Reproduced by permission of The Permissions Company, LLC on behalf of Carnegie Mellon University Press, www.cmu.edu/universitypress

SHARON OLDS: 'First Birth' from *Wellspring: Poems* by Sharon Olds, copyright © Sharon Olds, 1996. Reproduced by permission of Alfred A. Knopf, an imprint of the Knopf Doubleday Publishing Group, a division of Penguin Random House LLC. All rights reserved

PASCALE PETIT: 'Escape' from *Mama Amazonica*, Bloodaxe Books, 2017. Reproduced by permission of Bloodaxe Books, www.bloodaxebooks.com

JACKIE KAY: 'Chapter 2: The Original Birth Certificate' from *Darling: New & Selected Poems*, Bloodaxe Books, 2007. Reproduced by permission of the publisher, Bloodaxe Books, www.bloodaxebooks.com

NAN COHEN: 'A Newborn Girl at Passover' from *Rope Bridge*, Cherry Grove Collections, 2005. Reproduced by kind permission of the author

SYLVIA PLATH: 'Morning Song' from *Ariel*, in *Collected Poems* by Sylvia Plath, Faber and Faber Ltd, 2015. Reproduced by permission of the publisher

HOLLIE MCNISH: 'After Party/ After Birth' from *Plum*, Picador, 2017. Reproduced by permission of Lewinsohn Literary Limited

LIZ BERRY: 'The Republic of Motherhood' from *The Republic of Motherhood* by Liz Berry, Chatto & Windus, copyright © Liz Berry, 2018. Reproduced by permission of The Random House Group Limited

EAVAN BOLAND: 'Night Feed' from *New Selected Poems*, Carcanet, 2013. First published in *Poetry Ireland Review*, Issue 2. Reproduced by permission of Carcanet Press Limited and Poetry Ireland

HELEN DUNMORE: 'Patrick I' from *Counting Backwards: Poems 1975–2017*, Bloodaxe Books, 2019. Reproduced by permission of Bloodaxe Books, www.bloodaxebooks.com

RITA DOVE: 'Daystar' from *Collected Poems: 1974–2004* by Rita Dove, copyright © 1986 by Rita Dove. Reproduced by permission of W. W. Norton & Company, Inc.

KATHLEEN JAMIE: 'February' from *Book of Birth Poems*, Picador, 1999. Reproduced by permission of Jenny Brown Associates

DON PATERSON: 'Waking with Russell' from *Landing Light* by Don Paterson, Faber and Faber Ltd, 2004. Reproduced by permission of the publisher

ADA LIMÓN: 'Maybe I'll Be Another Kind of Mother' from *The Carrying*, Corsair, 2019. Reproduced by permission of Little, Brown Book Group Limited through PLSClear

SUSAN MEYERS: 'Mother, Washing Dishes' from *Keep and Give Away: Poems*, University of South Carolina Press, 2006. Reproduced by permission of University of South Carolina Press

SELIMA HILL: 'Mother Stone' from *Gloria: Selected Poems*, Bloodaxe Books, 2008. Reproduced by permission of Bloodaxe Books, www.bloodaxebooks.com

MATTHEW SIEGEL: 'Matthew you're leaving again so soon' from *Blood Work*, University of Wisconsin Press, 2015, copyright © the Board of Regents of the University of Wisconsin System, 2015. Reproduced by permission of the University of Wisconsin Press

MARY JEAN CHAN: 'postscript' from *Bright Fear* by Mary Jean Chan, Faber and Faber Ltd, 2023. Reproduced by permission of the publisher

PHILIP LARKIN: 'Mother, Summer, I' from *The Complete Poems* by Philip Larkin, Faber and Faber Ltd, 2012. Reproduced by permission of the publisher

NAOMI SHIHAB NYE: 'My Father and the Figtree' from *Words Under the Words: Selected Poems*, Far Corner Books 1994. Reproduced by permission of the author and publisher

LI-YOUNG LEE: 'The Gift' from *Rose*, copyright © Li-Young Lee, 1986. Reproduced by permission of The Permissions Company, LLC on behalf of BOA Editions, Ltd., boaeditions.org

ROBERT HAYDEN: 'Those Winter Sundays' from *Collected Poems of Robert Hayden* by Robert Hayden, ed. Frederick Glaysher, copyright © Robert Hayden, 1966. Reproduced by permission of Liveright Publishing Corporation

ROGER ROBINSON: 'Sleep' first published in *Out of Bounds: British Black and Asian Poets*, Bloodaxe Books, 2012 Reproduced by kind permission of the author

MALIKA BOOKER: 'The Little Miracles' first published in *Magma 75: The Loss Issue*, Spring 2020. Reproduced by kind permission of the author

ALISON BINNEY: 'Muscle Memory' from *The Opposite of Swedish Death Cleaning*, Seren Books, 2025. Reproduced by kind permission of the author

WAYNE HOLLOWAY-SMITH: 'The Posh Mums Are Boxing in the Square' from *Love Minus Love*, Bloodaxe Books, 2020. Reproduced by permission of Bloodaxe Books, www.bloodaxebooks.com

SEAMUS HEANEY: 'The Butts' from *Human Chain* by Seamus Heaney, Faber and Faber Ltd, 2012. Reproduced by permission of the publisher

RUTH FAINLIGHT: 'Handbag' from *New & Collected Poems*, Bloodaxe Books, 2010. Reproduced by permission of Bloodaxe Books, www.bloodaxebooks.com

RON CAREY: 'Upstairs' from *Distance*, Revival Press, copyright © Ron Carey. Reproduced by kind permission of the author

KAYO CHINGONYI: 'Kumukanda' from *Kumukanda* by Kayo Chingonyi, Chatto & Windus, 2017, copyright © Kayo Chingonyi, 2017. Reproduced by permission of The Random House Group Limited

E. E. CUMMINGS: 'if there are any heavens my mother will (all by herself) have' from *Portraits*, in *Complete Poems: 1904–1962* by E. E. Cummings, ed George J. Firmage, copyright © 1931, renewed 1959, 1991 by the Trustees for the E. E. Cummings Trust, copyright © George James Firmage, 1979. Reproduced by permission of Liveright Publishing Corporation

TONY HARRISON: 'Book Ends' from *Collected Poems* by Tony Harrison, Penguin Books, 2016. Reproduced by permission of Faber and Faber Ltd

OCEAN VUONG: 'Telemachus' from *Night Sky with Exit Wounds*, Jonathan Cape, copyright © Ocean Vuong, 2017. Reproduced by permission of The Random House Group Limited

LORNA GOODISON: 'My Mother's Sea Chanty' from *Collected Poems*, Carcanet, 2017. Reproduced by permission of Carcanet Press Limited

FAWZIA MURADALI KANE: 'Washing the Body' from *Guaracara*, Carcanet, 2025. Reproduced by permission of the author and Carcanet Press Limited

ANNE CARSON: 'Father's Old Blue Cardigan' from *Men in the Off Hours*, Vintage, 2001, copyright © Anne Carson, 2000. Reproduced by permission of The Random House Group Limited and Alfred A. Knopf, an imprint of the Knopf Doubleday Publishing Group, a division of Penguin Random House LLC. All rights reserved

ANNE SEXTON: 'All my Pretty Ones' from *The Complete Poems of Anne Sexton*, Houghton Mifflin, 1981, copyright © Linda Gray Sexton. Reproduced by permission of SLL/Sterling Lord Literistic, Inc.

EMILY BERRY: 'Canopy' from *Stranger, Baby* by Emily Berry, Faber and Faber Ltd, 2017. Reproduced by permission of the publisher

In some instances, we have been unable to trace the owners of copyright material, and we would appreciate any information that would enable us to do so. We would be pleased to correct any inadvertent errors or omissions.

INDEX OF AUTHORS

INDEX OF TITLES AND FIRST LINES